SOLDIER'S ARMOR
CHILDREN'S MILITARY & WAR HISTORY BOOKS

BABY PROFESSOR

EDUCATION KIDS

Armor is a protective covering that people wear to keep from getting hurt, or put on a vehicle to protect it. In war, soldiers\ wear armor so other soldiers have a harder time hurting them with their weapons. Armor can also protect people from damage that can be caused by a potentially dangerous environment. Soldiers and their war animals wear personal armor.

HISTORY OF THE USE OF ARMOR

Armor developed according to the need for it, and the resources available to make it. For example, plate armor first appeared in Medieval Europe, when water-powered trip hammers made the formation of plates faster and cheaper. The development of armor parallels the development of weapons. A stronger attack requires a better defense.

Armor has its limits: too much armor makes the wearer too slow and too awkward, so he can't fight back. The well-known types of armor in European history include the armor of the Roman legions: the lorica hamata, loricat segmentata, and lorica squamata. Later came the full steel plate harness worn by medieval knights and the mail hauberk of the early medieval age.

Heavy cavalry of several
European countries work
breast and back plates until
the first year of World War
I in 1914, when it was clear
the armor could not stop
modern bullets. In Japan,
samurai warriors wore many
types of armor for hundreds
of years, up to the 19th
century.

As early as the 4th century, helmets and breast plates were manufactured in Japan. Tankō was worn by foot soldiers while the keikō was worn by horsemen. These were both pre-samurai types of early Japanese armor that were constructed from iron plates connected with leather thongs.

Lamellar armor known as
keikō passed through Korea
and reached Japan in the
5th century. Early Japanese
lamellar armor has the form
of a sleeveless jacket and a
helmet. However, armor did
not always cover all of the
body. Sometimes soldiers
only war an armored helmet
and leg plates. A large shield
was generally used to protect
the rest of the body.

The ancient Greeks and the Aztecs from the 13th to the 15th centuries both equipped their troops in this fashion. In East Asia, there were many types of armor commonly used at different times by various cultures. They had brigandine, plate, scale and lamellar armor, and mail and plated mail. During the Song, Tang, and early Ming dynasties in China, cuirasses and plates (mingguangjia) were also used.

They had more elaborate
versions for the officers.
Instead of covering the whole
body, the Chinese used partial
plates for important body parts
since too much plate armor
made it hard to fight. They
covered the other body parts
in cloth, lamellar, leather, or
other materials. In the pre-Qin
dynasty, leather armor was
made out of various animals,
even more exotic ones like the
rhinoceros.

Mail, sometimes called chain mail, which was made of interlocking iron rings, first appeared sometime after 300 BC. The invention of this is credited to the Celts of England and France, and the Romans adopted the design.

Eventually, small additional discs of iron, or plates, were added to the mail to protect vulnerable areas. Splinted construction and hardened leather were used for arm and leg pieces. Armor made of large plates sewn inside a fabric or leather coat, known as a coat of plates, was developed.

From the 13th to the
15th century, plates in
Europe were made of
iron. Iron armor could
be carburized, or case-
hardened, to give it a hard
steel surface. Plate armor
became cheaper than mail
by the 15th century as it
required much less labor.
After the Black Death,
so many people had died
that labor became much
more expensive.

Mail continued to be used to protect areas which could not be protected by plate, like the groin, the armpit, and the elbow. An advantage of plate was that a lance rest could be fitted to the breast plate, to make it easier for the wearer to use his lance.

Small leather caps evolved into bigger true helmets, known as bassinets. The helmet was lengthened downward to protect the sides of the head and the back of the neck. Moreover, in the late 14th century, several new forms of helmets were introduced that were fully enclosed.

16TH CENTURY HEAVILY ARMORED RIDERS WITH BARDED WAR HORSES

The most recognized style of armor in the world is probably the plate armor associated with the knights of Europe in the late Middle Ages. Full harness of plate armor had been developed in the armories of Lombardy by about 1400.

Heavy cavalry had dominated the battlefield for centuries due in part because of their armor. Advances in weaponry allowed infantry to defeat armored knights on the battlefield in the early 15th century. As armies became bigger and armor was made thicker, the quality of the metal used in armor got worse.

Also, armor was heavy and required breeding of larger cavalry horses. Armor seldom weighed more than 15 kg during the 14th to15th centuries. But by the late 16th century, it weighed about 25 kg. The increased weight and thickness of the armor in the late 16th century gave substantial resistance to swords or arrows.

Breast plates or full suits of armor could actually stop bullets fired from a modest distance in the early years of low velocity firearms. Crossbow bolts would seldom penetrate good plate, nor would any other kind of bullet unless they were fired from close range. The use of firearms stimulated the development of plate armor into its later stages rather than making plate armor obsolete.

It allowed horsemen to fight while being the targets of defending harquebusiers without being easily killed for most of that period. Right up to the second decade of the 18th century, full suits of armor were worn by princely commanders and generals.

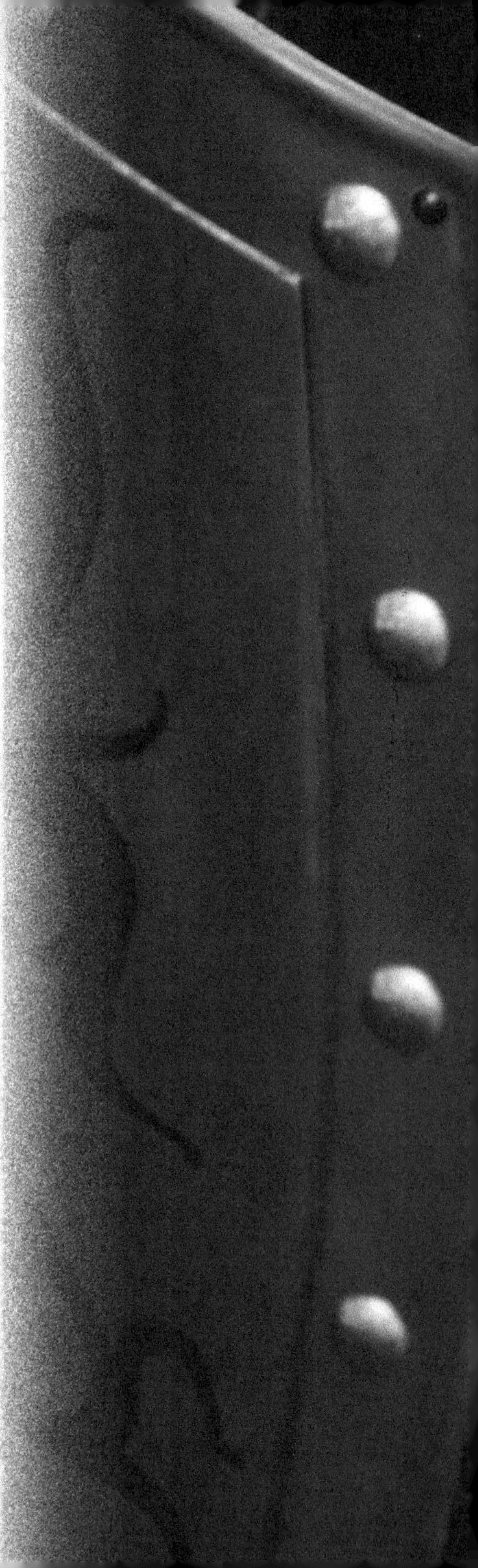

That was the only way they could be mounted and go around to survey the overall battlefield with safety against enemy musket fire.

———— ∞∞∞ ————

Did you enjoy reading? Don't forget to share this with your friends!

Visit

BABY PROFESSOR
EDUCATION KIDS

www.BabyProfessorBooks.com
to download Free Baby Professor eBooks and view
our catalog of new and exciting Children's Books